HOW TO INVEST IN THE STOCK MARKET

A Tutorial for the
Ultra-Beginner
Investor

F. Mike

2022 First Edition

Copyright © 2020
All rights reserved

How to Invest in the Stock Market:
A Tutorial for the Ultra-Beginner investor
By F. Mike

Disclaimer

The information provided by the author are for general informational purposes only and are not intended to provide specific financial advice or recommendations on any specific security. The publisher and author are providing this book and its contents on an "as is" basis and make no warranties or guarantees of any kind with respect to this book and its contents. In addition, the author and publisher assume no responsibility for errors, inaccuracies, or any other inconsistencies herein.

Contents

Chapter 1. What is investing

Chapter 2. Types of Stock Investment Vehicles

Chapter 3. Choose the Market Sector to Invest In

Chapter 4. Choose Your Investing Approach (Active and Passive)

Chapter 5. Choose Your Investment Focus (Growth and Value)

Chapter 6. Learn Investment Strategies

Chapter 7. How to Buy Your First Stock

Chapter 8. Tips to Help You Succeed

Chapter 9. Resources for Success

Chapter 10. Common Questions and Answers

Glossary

How to get the most from this book

This is a tutorial-style book that consists of specially selected topics with the goal of answering the questions that are most frequently asked by beginners in stock investing.

With this book, you will learn where and how to open your investment account and purchase your first stock. A notes section can be found at the end of some chapters for notetaking. This book also sheds some light on the commonly used terms in stock investing. The glossary contains an alphabetical list of words and their definitions for your reference as you read.

It is highly recommended that you read this tutorial to the end for a true understanding of what being a stock investor involves before you purchase stocks.

CHAPTER 1

What is Investing

Investing refers to the application of resources towards any venture that produces a gain. Woah! What was that? Why don't we drop the textbook lingo and chat like friends before I put us both to sleep? We will keep things simple and in the context of the stock market. Let us try that again. Simply put, investing is putting your money in anything that earns profit. For example, if you buy a pair of Nike shoes at $50 and sell them to your friend at $70, you have invested $50 into purchasing those Nike shoes. What makes the $50 an investment is that you applied it to something that earned you more money.

The Nike shoes are an asset. What makes the Nike shoes an asset is that they have earning potential, they were sold at a higher price than the purchase price, and they earned a profit, which in our example, is $20. If the Nike shoes had not been sold, but were instead, placed in a glass case to be admired with no intention of selling them, thus earning no money from them, the $50 spent to purchase them would not be an investment. It would be an expense, and the shoes would not be an asset. They would be a liability.

What is a liability you ask? Simply put, a liability is anything that costs money to acquire or maintain but does not earn money in return. For instance, if you buy a two hundred-thousand-dollar Bentley that does not earn you money through uber or other means, that Bentley is a liability. If you buy a one-thousand-dollar wig and it does not earn you money, that wig is a liability. As an investor, you should ask yourself before you make any major purchase if what you are about to purchase is an investment or a liability.

4 General Ways to Invest Your Money

Stock Ownership. You may invest your money by buying the stocks of a company. This will make you a part owner of the company also known as shareholder. As a shareholder, you may get dividends paid into your bank account by the company about 0-4 times in a year. Dividend is profit from a company that is distributed to shareholders. An investor can increase their ownership of a company by reinvesting their dividends into the company or by purchasing more shares of the company. Dividend reinvestment provides the opportunity to compound their investment. With compounding, the principal investment and interests generated grows additional wealth for the investor.

Interest Generating Savings Account. This refers to money placed in a savings account with any bank or credit union that will pay you interest for saving your money in their institution. If you have trouble keeping away from your savings account, you may put your money in an online savings account that has no or very few physical locations and some barriers to accessing your money. These barriers will go a long way to help you save.

Real Estate. You may invest your money by buying real estate. Real estate can be commercial, such as stores. They may also be residential, such as apartment buildings. You can earn income from real estate by collecting rent from your clients. You can also earn profit from real estate by selling the property at a higher price than your purchase and renovation costs.

Business. You may choose to invest your money by starting a business. For example, you may use your skills to do freelance work, teach a language that you are fluent in, begin selling items online, start a YouTube channel, start a landscaping business et cetera. Social media and Technology have made the process of starting a business much easier than it was in previous years. It has also become much easier to create and maintain multiple streams of income.

Why Choose the Stock Market Over an Interest Generating Savings Account?

Putting some of your cash in a bank account where it can generate interest is a brilliant idea. With an interest generating bank account your money will be insured up to $250,000. Which means, if the bank loses your money while it is in the interest generating bank account, you will be paid up to $250,000. This cash, however, is subject to inflation. Even with your interest earned on your cash, your money may be worth less than it was prior to you putting it in the savings account due to inflation. The best way to counter the effects of inflation is to 'grow' your money. That is where the stock market comes in. Before you go any further, you should evaluate yourself on whether you are cut out for stock investing. Remember, stock investing is only one type of investment. It is ok to decide that stock investing is not for you. Making this decision early in your investing journey will save you precious time and hard-earned money. There are many other ways to grow your money that do not involve the stock market. But before you decide against stock investing, you should know that investing in the stock market is one of the most passive ways that you can increase your wealth.

5 Signs You Will Absolutely Hate Stock Investing

1. You are impatient. Wealth growth takes time. Increasing your wealth through stock investing is more like a slow chug over many years than a sprint. Time is an essential part of the process. The earlier you begin investing in the stock market, the higher your chances of growing substantial wealth. This is even more so when compounding is utilized. The longer the length of time an investor stays invested in a dividend paying stock, the better their chances of compounding the dividends earned.

2. You hate taking risks and cannot stand the thought of losing any money. You must embrace the very real possibility that you may lose your money to the market. Otherwise, you are not ready. The market can be quite brutal to inexperienced investors that lack foresight and direction. Research and focus can go a long way to enable you make smarter and safer investment decisions and minimize monetary loss.

3. You are prone to FOMO (Fear of Missing Out). FOMO can lead one to make hasty decisions without proper research. This can

be a financial disaster especially for beginner investors with little money. After you have decided on whether to invest in a company based on your research, it is important that you are not swayed by the actions of others. Investors have different strategies for investing in a particular company, so imitating another investor without knowing their 'why' may be detrimental to you.

4. You are bad at predicting human behavior. The stock market and the economy in general are controlled by lots of factors such as the political climate, weather, natural disaster, epidemic, pandemic, and most importantly, human behavior. The easier it is for you to predict general human behavior in different economic climates, the easier it will be for you to predict the direction of a particular stock.

5. You lack common sense. Listen, this is tough love. You are still an amazing person and we all still love you. However, if you find yourself repeatedly, the key word here is repeatedly, making costly mistakes in ANY aspect of your life, then it is safe to say that you lack common sense. To succeed in stock investing, you need common sense like humans need oxygen. Common sense will be a reoccurring theme throughout the rest of this book.

How to Increase Your Net Worth Using Stocks

Increasing your net worth through stocks can be accomplished in 3 broad ways: through stock price appreciation, dividends, and by increasing ownership of a company by increasing the number of the company's shares you own.

1. **Stock price appreciation.** This refers to an increase in the price of a stock. Buying a stock when the price is down and selling it when the price increases, is one way to earn money from the stocks that you own. While this is a clever idea, it is sometimes best to buy a stock and hold it for an extended period as stock prices tend to increase over longer periods. For example, there are investors that purchased Amazon stocks when it was $50 and sold it when it reached $500. While they made a sweet 10x return on their investment, if they held it long enough until, say, July 2021 they would have made an even sweeter 70x return on their investment when Amazon stocks were priced at $3500.

2. **Dividends.** Another way to increase your net worth through owning stocks is by receiving dividends. Dividends are profits distributed by a company to its shareholders. Owning a share or company stock makes you

a shareholder of that company. Companies that pay dividends make quarterly or annual payments to their shareholders which the shareholders may either use to fund their lifestyle or reinvest into buying more stocks to increase their ownership of the company. Many companies do not pay dividends to their shareholders. For example, technology stocks such as Amazon, Apple, and Tesla. Therefore, if you decide that you want to be a dividend investor, do careful research to ensure that you are selecting companies that pay dividends to their shareholders.

3. Increasing ownership of a particular company. A straightforward way to accomplish this is by gradually increasing the number of stocks of a particular company that you own. If on a bi-weekly or monthly basis, when your employer pays you for your 9-5 employment, you purchase a couple of stocks from company xyz, you are slowly increasing the number of the company's stock you own and therefore, increasing your ownership of company xyz. This method is referred to as dollar-cost averaging. You may have noticed that if you purchase stocks on a schedule, say, after every pay period, some of your stock purchases are likely to fall on a day when the stock prices are high. However, if regular stock purchases are maintained, you will gradually grow your money and minimize the risk that comes with trying to perfectly time the market to purchase stocks at the perfectly low price or at the bottom. It is highly improbable to perfectly time the market with every purchase. One disadvantage to dollar-cost averaging is that the market rises over time, hence, buying stocks when the price is at its lowest with a lump sum could result in higher return over time. Always remember, with higher returns come greater risk!

Common Mistakes New Investors Make

1. Procrastinate. Many new investors wait too long before taking their first step towards owning stocks. This may be because they are intimidated by the stock market. Hence, they decide to learn as much as possible about the market before investing their hard-earned money. The delay could also be due to analysis paralysis. This is a circumstance whereby; a person is stuck in their research and analysis stage as they try to learn all that there is to know about the subject and solve every potential problem for such a prolonged period that they never act. A solution to this is recognizing that some unpredictability is okay, and a positive result is still achievable without knowing everything there is to know about the stock market.

2. Invest in a company they do not understand. Some new investors buy stocks without a sufficient understanding of the company's goals, forecasts, or a good knowledge of the goods and services that company provides. For example, a person that has basic knowledge of Amazon as the seller hub that is Amazon.com may consider Walmart, another large and popular seller hub, to be a bigger competitor and a better investment choice because they are not aware of Amazon's cloud business called Amazon Web Service (AWS) or its space travel program called Blue Origin and how they play a significant role in Amazon's stock prices and brand as a whole. In-depth research about a company prior to investing is vital to choosing the right company. Information on where to go to research a company is provided in subsequent chapters. Remember to avoid analysis paralysis while performing research.

3. Buying a company's stocks simply because they 'like' the company or use their products. Many new investors fail to realize that a company that has a good public image and good products may be a terrible investment E.g., Enron, and a company that has a less positive image may be a worthwhile investment E.g., Johnson & Johnson. Some companies have withstood the test of time by thriving in many recessions and periods of

market volatility. The ability of a company to grow and expand during many unpleasant market conditions can be proof of its strength and dependability for investing.

4. Buy and sell stocks based on emotion. Many new investors become afraid and sell when stock prices fall. New investors often do the opposite of what they should during a downturn by selling a good stock when its price falls. This is like choosing to buy a Rolex when the price is high and refusing to buy it when it goes on sale. A stock should be purchased when its price is low and sold when high. Holding unto a stock while its price falls is easier said than done. It takes resilience and determination on the part of the new investor.

5. Invest in a company's stock simply because their favorite billionaire is invested in that company. Many new investors are not aware that the billionaire investors they mimic have more complex investment strategies. Hence, their investment styles may not necessarily work for the new investor. Successful investors may be considered as inspiration for the new investor. However, the inexperienced investor must have a goal and work toward achieving it while recognizing that their investment strategy may or may not be the same as that of their favorite billionaire investor.

6. Inflexibility in investment style (short-term vs long-term investing). Many new investors stick to their chosen investment style of being short-term investors or long-term investors for a particular stock. For example, if a stock is purchased to be held long-term or for many years, but after a few months, the investor learns of information that shows that investing long-term with the company will result in a loss, they remain inflexible in their chosen style. It is okay to sell the stock to avoid losing money. Do not hold on to a "bad" stock for the long-term just because you define yourself strictly as a long-term investor.

7. Buying when everyone else is buying. As a stock investor, you want to buy stocks when the prices are lower than they usually are. To do so successfully, you need to buy stocks before the rest of the public catch on and begin purchasing, as this can cause the stock's price to increase. If an investor buys stocks when everybody else is doing so, it is highly likely that the investor is buying them at a high price not a low price. The key to successfully buying stocks before the prices increase is staying up to date with news about the market and the company in question. Reading market news, company newsletters, and company's earnings reports will keep the new investor current on market news.

CHAPTER 2

Types of Stock Investment Vehicles

Bringing our conversation back to the stock market, there are 4 investment vehicles that you need to grow wealth. You may use one or more of them. The investment vehicles are as follows:

1. Individual stocks. A stock is a part of a company. Therefore, by purchasing stocks from a company, you are purchasing a part of that company. This makes you a part owner of the company. Owning individual stocks can provide great returns for the investor when the company grows, expands, and its stock prices increase, or when dividends are paid. However individual stocks come with risks as do all other investment types. Individual stocks may be held either long-term or short-term. One example of an individual stock is Coca Cola which has the ticker symbol KO. A ticker symbol is a symbol that represents the assets or securities of a publicly traded company.

2. Mutual funds. This refers to an investment system whereby, funds from several people are pooled together to invest in different areas such as stocks, bonds, real estate, or commodities. One mutual fund may include assets from thousands of companies. This type of investment ranks high in diversification. Diversification in investment is important because it can significantly reduce the risk associated with investing. The investor in a mutual fund owns a portion of the securities that the fund is invested in. The fund's manager actively manages mutual funds. Mutual funds are better suited for long-term investments as this allows more time for the investment to offset the fees that are deducted from the investment gains.

3. Exchange Traded Funds (ETF). An ETF is a group of stocks or bond, as many as thousands, in a single fund. An ETF is traded on a major stock exchange such as Nasdaq and the New York Stock Exchange. They are highly diversified because there are tens, hundreds, or even thousands of stocks or bonds in one ETF. They have lower fees when compared to mutual funds. They are less work for the investor as they are managed by the fund managers and their diversified nature make them less risky than individual stocks. An example of an ETF is Vanguard's total world stock which has the ticker symbol, VT.

4. Index funds. These are funds that comprise of a group of stocks and bonds in a single fund that tracks a particular index such as the S&P 500 or the Nasdaq Composite Index. The S&P 500 Index is a group of the top 500 companies in the U.S. that acts as a performance tracker. The index tracks market performance while an index fund, for example, SPY index fund by Fidelity tracks the S&P 500 index. The Nasdaq composite is group of about 3000 common stocks that tracks market performance. The Nasdaq is dominated by technology stocks followed by consumer services and healthcare. Index funds are like ETFs in that they are highly diversified assets in a fund. Fund managers manage index funds, and they have some of the lowest fees. Index fund managers work to match the performance of the index that the fund tracks.

Investing in index funds, like ETFs and mutual funds can be quite passive for the investor. The investor can simply add to their position by purchasing more of a particular index fund, mutual fund, or ETF, or simply holding what they have for an extended period. The investor does not have to seek out or contact an investment manager or notify the brokerage company of their purchase as they are simply buying into an already existing fund which is being managed by the fund managers. Index funds and mutual funds are not traded as often as individual funds. Hence, if an investor wishes to trade often i.e., trade multiple times in one market day, then index funds, mutual funds, and ETFs are not the best opinion.

The information in the figure below comprises of the general features of the funds described and may be different depending on factors such as brokerage firm, funds class, and other factors. Once your brokerage account is created with a brokerage company, any funds purchase you make within the brokerage account is automatically managed by the fund managers, although, decisions regarding which funds to own still lies with the investor. The exception to this is when individual stocks are purchased. In this case, it is the responsibility of the investor to decide whether to buy, hold or sell those stocks. If the investor buys an individual stock and does nothing else after that, the stock is automatically held in the investor's account and grows either through increasing stock prices, dividend yields, or both. The money invested may be lost if there is a market downturn or if the company goes bankrupt. In other words, with investing, no action is an action!

Note that diversification can be achieved by purchasing individual stocks from different sectors of the stock market, However, this method of investing and the level of research required to achieve effectiveness may be too complex for the new investor.

Individual Stocks vs Index Funds vs Mutual Funds vs ETFs

Features	Individual stock	Index fund	Mutual fund	ETF
No. of companies in each	One	Many	Many	Many
Tracks	Nothing	An index	An index	An asset or index
Professionally pooled/managed	No	Yes	Yes	Yes
Active or Passive	Can be both	Generally passive	Generally active	Generally passive
Trades executed	Day + Ext hours	Once, after market close	Once, after market close	Day + Ext hours
Trading fees	None/Low	None/Low	High	Low
Diversified	No	Yes	Yes	Yes
Relative risk level	High	Low	Low	Low

Figure 1: the table below is a comparison of some of the features of individual stocks, index funds, mutual funds, and ETFs.

Quick tip: if you do not feel comfortable with choosing the right individual stocks or trading frequently, or you have a 9-5 job and cannot dedicate many hours to frequent trades throughout the day, you may choose the passive and diversified route by buying an index fund, a mutual fund, or an ETF. Most of the time, passively managed funds that track an index outperforms actively managed funds and individually picked stocks.

Notes:

CHAPTER 3

Choose the Market Sector to Invest In

1. Information Technology. These stocks are from companies that participate in the production of electronic goods and their components such as hardware, software, semiconductor equipment, communication equipment, as well as information technology (IT) services. Examples of an ETF and a stock in the information technology sector are Vanguard Information Technology (VGT) and Apple (AAPL).

2. Healthcare. This sector includes companies that are in the business of providing products and services related to healthcare. The goods and services may include pharmaceuticals, hospitals, rehabilitation centers, vaccines, medical equipment, animal shelters, and nursing homes. Examples of an ETF and a stock in this sector are Fidelity MSCI Healthcare Index ETF (FHLC) and Moderna (MRNA).

3. Real Estate. This sector includes companies that participate in the exploration, acquisition, and sale of real estate properties. Property types may include offices, warehouses, residential buildings, retail centers, medical facilities, hotels, cell towers, and infrastructure. Examples of an ETF and a stock in this sector are Schwab US REIT ETF (SCHH) and Public Storage (PSA).

4. Energy. These stocks include companies that perform development, and production of oil refining and biofuels, petroleum exploration, oil and gas drilling, coal mining, wind power generation, and renewable energy such as hydropower. Examples of an ETF and a stock in the energy industry are Invesco Solar ETF (TAN), and Chevron Corporation (CVX).

5. Consumer Staples. This sector includes companies that participate in the manufacturing and distribution of food, tobacco, beverages, personal products, and other household goods such as laundry detergents, snacks, toilet paper et cetera. The goods produced in this sector are not sensitive to economic cycles. Hence, the stocks in this sector are called defensive stocks. Defensive stocks are stocks that can provide consistent earnings regardless of the state of the stock market. This is possible because the goods produced are needed regardless of the state of the stock market. Examples of an ETF and a stock in this sector are Vanguard Consumer Staples (VDC) and Proctor and Gamble (PG).

6. Consumer discretionary. These stocks are from companies that produce appliances, entertainment, et cetera. These comprises goods that are considered non-essential. As a result, they are cyclical stocks. Cyclical stocks fluctuate readily in response to market conditions. Due to their nature as goods that people want rather than need, consumers spend more on them when market conditions are positive, and less money on them when the economy is down. Examples of an ETF and a stock in this sector are Consumer Discretionary Select Sector SPDR Fund (XLY) and LOWE'S (LOW).

7. Materials. This sector includes companies that produce construction materials like cement or metal; packaging materials like plastic, cardboard; and glass, mining materials like copper, gold, silver or aluminum, and forest products such as paper and lumber. Examples of an ETF and a stock in this sector are Vanguard Materials ETF (VAW) and Air Products and Chemicals (APD).

8. Industrials. This sector includes companies that produce construction and manufacturing equipment, aerospace and defense, waste management, electrical equipment, as well as transportation services such as airport and railway operations. Examples of an ETF and a stock in this sector are iShares US Industrials ETF (IYJ) and Waste Management (WM).

9. Utilities. This sector includes companies that distribute electricity, gas, water, and renewable energy. The stocks in this sector are defensive stocks because they do not respond readily to market fluctuations. People need electricity, water, and gas regardless of the market's conditions. Examples of an ETF and a stock in this sector are Invesco S&P 500 Equal Weight Utilities ETF (RYU) and Aqua America (WTRG).

10, Financial Services This sector includes companies that provide financial services to people and corporations. Financial services include banking services, mortgage services, investment services, tax and accounting services, and insurance services. Examples of an ETF and a stock in this sector are Vanguard Financial ETF (VFH) and Berkshire Hathaway (BRK.A) (BRK.B).

11. Communication Services. This sector includes companies that make communication possible globally either through phones or internet, via wires or wirelessly, audio, or video, and data transfer and interpretations. Examples of an ETF and a stock in this sector are Fidelity MSCI Communication Services ETF (FCOM) and Facebook (FB).

3 Broad Categories of Market Sectors

Understanding the structure of the stock market will allow you to properly diversify your investment portfolio such that you are not too heavily weighted in one sector of the market while missing out in other sectors. It is advantageous to be invested in the three broad categories of the stock market to lower your risk and increase your earnings potential regardless of the state of the market. The three categories are:

1. Cyclical: companies in this category are extremely sensitive to market volatility. Many companies in this sector produce goods that fulfill wants rather than the needs of consumers. Here, your earnings are high when the market is up, and low when the market is down. Cyclical stocks are not inherently poor investment choices because of their sensitivity, to market conditions. The investor will have to be more risk tolerant when investing in cyclical stocks during volatile market conditions. Companies in this category may include companies in the automotive, fashion, and furniture industries.

2. Defensive: companies in this category are not sensitive to market volatility. Here, your earnings are not affected by market volatility because the goods and products are essential.

Defensive stocks are typically stocks of companies that sell products that people need to buy regularly. This also means that during periods of inflation, when prices of goods are high, consumers may decide to cut back on their purchases, which may in turn affect the revenue of these companies, and in turn, their stock prices. Companies in this category may include companies in the food, gasoline, and healthcare industries.

3. Moderate Sensitivity: companies in this category are moderately affected by market volatility. Hence, earnings can be affected by market fluctuations, but not as much as in the cyclical category. Some companies in the entertainment industry fall in this category. One could also argue that Testa falls in this category as they are perceived by consumers as both a technology company and an automotive company. There are many companies that do not fall neatly in the categories listed above especially due to the interconnections of technology into virtually every industry in today's market.

The broad categories of stock market sectors are summarized in the table below to show how human needs and behavior interact with the stock market. With this information, a new investor can decide on which sector of the market to invest in during volatile and non-volatile periods. This information can also be used to predict the behavior of other investors in different economic conditions.

Cyclical	Defensive	Moderate Correlation
Real Estate	Healthcare	Information Technology
Consumer Discretionary	Consumer Staples	Energy
Materials	Utilities	Industrials
Financials		Communication Services

Figure 2: The table above shows which sectors of the market falls under the cyclical, defensive and moderate correlation with market conditions.

Quick tip: Cyclical stocks perform very well when purchased in a down market. Taking advantage of market fluctuations can speed up the growth of your wealth. Defensive stocks perform well in different market conditions. They reduce the risk of losing money when the market is down. Therefore, diversifying will help you maximize your earnings.

Notes:

CHAPTER 4

Choose Your Investing Approach

There are two main ways to approach investing, actively or passively. For the benefit of the audience for which this book is written, we will define an active investment as an investment method that involves active strategizing and trading of assets by the investor. This includes skilled and unskilled stock investors. We will define passive investing as an investing style that does not involve active strategizing and trading of assets by the investor. Making this distinction is important because there are advantages and disadvantages to choosing to be an active or a passive investor. As a new investor that has regular employment and is required to be physically present at work within certain periods of time throughout the week, or if you have a family that demands your attention, or you have limited capital, you may want to know what these two investing styles will require.

1. Active Investing. This type of investor holds stock for a shorter period than a passive investor. Their duration for holding stocks could be as short as a few minutes to a few weeks. The active investor engages in market analysis, stock chart interpretations, and frequent trading to increase their gains and minimize their losses. If you decide to be a self-directed investor, you may choose to be an active investor. An active investor has a more hands-on approach towards their investment portfolio and have a deep understanding of the economy and politics. With this type of investing, the investor plays a more active role in choosing the assets they want to invest in. This allows them to have more control over the stocks in their portfolio. A successful active investor must understand the market and how it responds to the social, political, and economic climate. They must be knowledgeable in interpreting market chart data, they must have the ability to obtain current news, and act quickly to take advantage of any market volatility that might occur. An active investor may also be a day trader who trades stocks multiple times within a day. With day trading, it is extremely important that the investor stays current on news that affect their investment or the economy.

Tax laws often differ for active investing compared to passive investing. While some active investors hold their investments for a prolonged period, others such as day traders do not. Hence a day trader may generate more capital gains in a brief period than the investor that holds their stock for a longer time. The new investor should know capital gains generated from short-term investments are taxed at higher rates than capital gains generated from long-term investments. Capital gains simply means the returns from the sale of an asset. Gains from an investment that was held for less than one year is considered short-term capital gains, while gains from an investment that was held for more than one year are considered long-term gains. Regarding investing fees, an active investor that does not pick their stocks themselves may be required to pay fees such as administrative fees and performance fees due to their use of the expertise of fund managers that actively perform the trades. Examples of actively managed investments are investment portfolios managed by professional portfolio managers. The goal of an active investor is to outpace the index's return or beat the market's return. Some highly intelligent and experienced investors have been known to succeed at achieving this for a few years, but eventually, the market always wins.

2. Passive Investing. This is the most common method utilized by new investors with little money. A passive investor applies the buy and hold strategy by buying stocks and holding them for an extended period, from years to decades, while allowing their value to increase. Passive investments do not typically outperform the market. They usually mirror the market's performance. So, if the market has a difficult year, so will the investment. The goal of a passive investment is to get the index's return. Passive investors typically buy and hold index funds and ETFs although many also buy and hold mutual funds and individual stocks. Due to the nature of the passive investor's investing style, they have less control over what type of stocks are in a particular ETF. A single ETF may have as many as 500 company's stocks. With passive investing, the investor does not need to know the ins and outs of the economy at the same capacity that the active investor does. With basic investing knowledge, the passive investor can successfully utilize resources to increase their wealth.

Passive investments are typically taxed at a lower rate because they are held for longer periods of time. A passive investor that buys an asset, makes some gains, but changes their mind and sells the asset after less than a year of holding the asset will be taxed at the rate for short-term investments if capital gains are realized from the investment. Passive investments are typically less expensive than active investments as there are less taxes for the investor. An individual investor that picks index funds for themselves may only need to pay the expense ratio, which is an exceedingly small percentage, sometimes as low as 0.02% annually for the operational cost of the fund. A passive investor that is an individual stock picker does not pay any annual fees. Most fees for individual stock picking have been waived by brokerage firms to stay competitive. Index funds, mutual funds, and ETFs have expense ratios, individual stocks do not. So, an individual can purchase stocks and hold them for a prolonged period as they increase in value and pay no fees. Yes, Zero fees! An example of a passive investment is an individual that buys an index fund and holds it for an extended period.

The goal of a passive investor is to mirror the market's performance through the buy and hold strategy using individual stocks, index funds, mutual funds, and ETFs. Since the market eventually wins, passive investing is often more successful than any other investment style. Active investing is not beyond the capabilities of a new investor. However, it is more involved in terms of the number of actions the investor will need to take. Both types of investing have their advantages and disadvantages as summarized in the table below.

Pros and Cons of Active vs Passive Investing

Features	Active Investing	Passive Investing
Market data analysis	Requires more.	Requires less.
Investor control	Investor has more control	Investor has less control
Investor time	Demands more time.	Demands less time.
Fees	More fees paid.	Less fees paid.
Capital Gains Tax over a short time	Higher	Lower
Long-run success rate	Lower.	Higher.
Probability of trading at the wrong time	High	Low
Relative probability of getting an average return	Low	High
Challenging	More	Less
Outperform the market	More likely	Less likely

Figure 3: A comparison of active and passive investing. Note that this is a generalization of both types of investing. There are more distinction and overlaps than the table shows. This table assumes that the active investor engages in frequent trades and the passive investor does not. The table focuses on few important aspects of investing such as control, time demands, fees and taxes.

Investment Duration for the Passive Investor

Knowing the duration of time that you plan to hold onto your investments is important because it allows you to plan your investment strategies.

1. Short-term investment. This refers to a strategy that allows for the investment to be readily converted to cash and the investor intends to convert it to cash within a few months to a few years. It also refers to investments that are held for up to one year. These time frames are not set in stone. Besides tax situations, what is short-term for one investor may be considered long-term for another. Short-term investing gives the investor the opportunity to take advantage of the rises and dips that the stock will experience. For instance, if you buy a stock and the price of the stock rises initially but later begins to decline, you can sell that stock before the price drops too low. Thereby, eliminating the risk of losing your money.

If, say, two months after you have sold your position, the stock drops even further, and you believe that the stock is going to rise soon, you can repurchase the stock at the much lower price and hold it until the price increases before selling the stock. This is one way that you can take advantage of the rise and fall of a stock's price in the short-term. This may be easier said than done as it requires that you have a deeper understanding of the market and the company. You will also need to be adept at making educated guesses and forecasts on the behavior and price of the stock for you to be successful. Remember, every time you earn capital gains from selling, you create a taxable event for which you will need to pay taxes in the form of a capital gains tax during tax season.

2. Long term investment. This refers to holding an investment for about 1 year or longer. A long-term investor typically buys and holds their investment as they do not intend to sell in the short-term. This gives their investments an opportunity to grow. As a long-term investor, you can take advantage of drops in stock prices by buying more of that stock while the price is down. This is a useful method if you depend on your employment for funds with which you use to invest. For instance, if you purchase the Vanguard Technology ETF (VGT) but you could only afford to buy one, you may decide to save some money from your paychecks in an interest generating bank account until you accumulate enough money to afford another VGT. When you have enough money, you can purchase a second VGT to add to your position. Simply repeat this process until you have the number of VGTs you would like in your portfolio or continue the process indefinitely until retirement or until you decide to liquidate your position to make a major purchase such as a piece of property.

If you invest long-term, your investments may experience some drops in prices in a market cycle as that is normal. However, if you have picked a good company, you can be comfortable in knowing that the stock price will increase in the future. If you do not do sufficient research on the company you invest in, you stand the risk of the company's stock prices falling to zero and losing all your money. Remember, the money that you put in the stock market is not insured and losing all your money is a very real possibility.

3. Fluid term investment. This is a term coined by yours truly. It refers to an investment style that allows you to switch from short-term investment to long-term investment or vice-versa when the situation calls for it. As simple as this sounds, many investors remain rigidly in their predetermined investment duration despite the potential for a more favorable outcome with a different investment duration. For example, if you bought a stock with the intention of holding it short-term, however, you learned that the company will be expanding their customer base by acquiring another company, you may decide not to sell your position in the short-term, but to hold onto it and add more to your position when the opportunity arises because you know that the company will be more successful in the long-term.

On the other hand, if you own stocks in a company that you intend to hold long-term, however, you learn of the company's fraudulent revenue reporting practices and a possible investigation of the company, you may decide to sell your stocks instead of holding onto a stock that may fall to zero. What is most important is knowing when to hold and when to sell a position.

Quick tip: since both active and passive investing have their unique advantages, to maximize your returns from stock investing, consider a combination of both.

Notes:

CHAPTER 5

Choose Your Investment Focus

There are two primary areas of focus for investors when deciding on which companies to invest in. The two primary areas are growth and value. These are not mutually exclusive. Hence, some companies will have elements of both. Learning these two categories will help you recognize which category a particular company falls under when you are performing research on the companies you would like to invest in. The two categories are as follows:

1. Growth investing. This is an approach to investing whereby, the investor focuses on investing in companies that they believe will continue to grow at a rate faster than other companies in its sector. A growth investor will buy growth stocks even if it is trading above average price or considered expensive because the investor believes that the stock price will continue to appreciate. The stock prices of growth stocks are usually more expensive than other types of stocks because of the widely held belief that these companies will continue to grow well into the future and the stock prices will continue to increase. Growth companies offer significant potential for the investor to increase their wealth because the companies are growing. This also means that growth companies are inherently riskier. There is no guarantee that the company will continue to grow and be profitable. Growth companies do not typically pay dividends to their investors. Their cash flow is reinvested into the company to take advantage of growth opportunities.

Although growth companies focus on growth, that does not mean that the companies are not valuable companies. Being a growth company simply means that the company demonstrates potential for higher-than-average earnings. These types of companies may outperform the market during periods of high or low economic growth, but they may also perform worse than the market during periods of slow economic growth. Many growth companies performed well during the 2020-2022 economic downturn. A growth investor may invest short-term and make significant gains because growth companies are actively growing, and their stock prices experience much volatility. Price volatility creates many opportunities for the investors to either add to their positions or trade in and out of their positions while growing their money in the process. Remember that while growth investing has a higher potential for great returns, they also have greater risk. An example of growth companies are companies in the technology sector such as Amazon and Tesla.

2. Value investing. This refers to an investing style that focuses on acquiring stocks for their intrinsic value. The intrinsic value of a company is a measure of what the company is worth based on the product or service it provides. A value investor will usually buy stocks of undervalued companies and hold them long-term as they wait for the prices to increase. Companies that are considered for value investing are typically well-established companies that are perceived to be undervalued. Their stocks are usually less expensive relative to other stocks, which is no surprise as they are undervalued. Cashflow generated by value companies are either paid as dividends to their shareholders or put towards the expansion of the company. Value stocks are less risky than other types of stocks because they are usually businesses that have been shown to generate profit.

As a value investor who holds stocks long term, the investor must be prepared to withstand any market volatility that might bring lower stock prices in the normal market cycles and be determined enough to withstand FOMO (Fear of Missing Out) which may lead the investor to panic and sell their positions before they ought to. Selling a value investment too soon or in short-term defeats the purpose of value investing because the gains from value investing will not be realized in the short-term. It takes time for an undervalued company whose stock prices are lower than the perceived intrinsic value to begin to trade at their intrinsic value. Hence, a value investor must be prepared to hold onto their value stock for a prolonged period, sometimes decades, to realize the gains they desire. An example of value companies are companies in the consumer staples sector such as General Mills Inc. (GIS) and Proctor and Gamble (PG).

Please note that the concept of a growth company versus a value company is subjective to the investor. Investor A may consider Intuitive Surgical (ISRG) to be a value company if they believe that it is undervalued based on the product and service that it provides and the direction that artificial intelligence is taking robotic surgery. Investor B may consider Intuitive Surgical a growth company based on its perceived growth potential. If both investors purchase ISRG stocks and investor A treats it like a value stock and investor B treats it like a growth stock, both investors will reap the benefits of the style of investing they employ. The investor's understanding, interpretation, and application of definitions and rules is what is most important in growing your portfolio and wealth. There is often no right and wrong answer in investing. You must however stay educated, informed, and focused on achieving your goals. This brings us to a critical point made earlier which is that, following your favorite investor's investments by buying what they buy and selling when they sell may not be the best option for you because their goals and interpretations may be different from yours.

Comparison of Growth vs Value Stocks

	Growth stocks	Value stocks
Investor's focus	Growth potential	Intrinsic value
Affordability	More expensive	Less expensive
Ways to grow wealth	Capital appreciation	Dividends/capital appreciation
Risk level	Higher	Lower
Pays dividends	Typically, no	Typically, yes
Stock appreciation	Yes	Yes
Investment duration	Long or short-term	Long term

Figure 4: A comparison between growth and value stocks. This table reflects what is most typical of the two types of stocks.

Quick tip: a combination of both growth and value investing will give you benefits of both types of investing and help you minimize risk in different market conditions.

Notes:

CHAPTER 6

Learn Investment Strategies

Here are some simple and straightforward strategies that will assist you in your investing journey.

1. Set goals. your goal does not have to be an amount of money. It could be freedom from a 9 to 5 job, more control over your schedule, freedom to travel, and many more. The point of setting a goal is to put into perspective, how much work is ahead of you and how much time you will need to accomplish your goal. You may also set short-term goals such as how many funds you need to own before the end of the year. An even shorter-term goal could be how much money you need to save to buy your first stock.

2. Consider indexing. Buying index funds, mutual funds, or ETFs is a very passive and beginner friendly investment path. It is one of the safest stock investing strategies that exists. It can easily be automated such that, an amount of money is automatically transferred from your checking account to your brokerage account and used to purchase stocks with the help of a robo-advisor. Although as a beginner investor, it is best that you be more hands-on with your money transfers and stock purchases as that will help you to understand the investing process at a deeper level.

3. Consider dividend growth investing. Buying dividend stocks is an opportunity for compounding growth. Compounding growth is a process whereby additional earnings are generated from the reinvestment of the earnings from an investment. Remember that compounding is only possible when your earnings are reinvested or by buying more stocks. Earning do not have to be reinvested. They can be received quarterly as income.

4. Asset Allocation. Some assets are more volatile than others. Be aware of which assets are more prone to market volatility before you invest your money in them. See figure 2 for a refresher on which assets are more prone to market volatility. Be aware of how much of your money is invested in volatile assets and how much are in safer assets. Generally, volatile assets grow your money faster, but you are less likely to lose your money with less volatile assets. Therefore, a balance of both will be wise.

5. Diversify, diversify, diversify. Diversification means investing in more than one sector. It reduces your risk of losing money and increases your chances of achieving higher growth. Diversification does not always mean buying many diverse types of funds or stocks. An investor can be diversified with just one fund. E.g., the Vanguard Total World Stock (VT) is a diversified fund that contains stocks from all the sector of the economy. It also includes international stocks. Yes! You can buy just VT consistently and have a diversified portfolio.

6. Choose low-cost investments. Know how much your investments will cost you in the form of administrative or broker fees. You will not pay broker fees if you do not use a broker. A broker is a person that buys and sells assets for others, in this case, a person that trades stocks for others. Load fees (a.k.a broker fees) are charged when you buy or sell some mutual funds. You will not pay load fees if you do not purchase funds that have them. Expense ratios are charged on ETFs and are shown as percentages that are charged annually. These percentages should not be interpreted as dollar amounts, but earnings percentages of investments. A 2% expense ratio can be a lot of money. There are many funds with extremely low expense ratios. You do not need to buy funds with high expense ratios.

7. Add to your winners. This means exactly what it says. When you purchase a stock for the long term and it is performing well, it will benefit you to purchase more of that stock to increase your position (the amount of that stock you own). This will allow you to reap the maximum benefit of owning a bigger portion of a stock that is performing well. If you decide to time the market by waiting until the stock prices fall to make a purchase, you may be putting yourself at a disadvantage because perfectly timing the market is more difficult than it seems and can lead to slower growth eventually.

8. Invest regularly. Remember, if your money is not being invested, it is being spent on liabilities or lost to inflation. Your growth will compound automatically when you invest regularly. An advantage to investing regularly is that, instead of investing a generous sum, you can afford to invest tiny amounts of money that can increase overtime. It also allows you to learn about investing as you go rather than jumping into an investment with all your savings before you have experienced different market cycles. Investing should be more of a lifestyle than a one and done occurrence.

9. You may save up to your investment. Some funds may be above your immediate affordability. It is ok to save up to buy those funds. Saving to buy a fund is not different from saving up to buy an Xbox or an expensive purse. If you can hold onto your tax refund from the beginning of the year until Black Friday to buy your favorite 75-inch tv, then you can apply the same behavior towards investing by holding onto your tax refund until you identify a good company to invest in.

10. Use dollar-cost averaging. You could use dollar cost averaging to reduce the negative impact of volatility of the market on your portfolio. This means buying stocks with equal amounts of money at regular intervals regardless of the price of the fund. It eliminates the possibility of buying funds with a large amount of money when the prices are high. Dollar-cost averaging does not have to be the only system applied. For instance, in March of 2020 at the height of the pandemic, it would have been more advisable to make large purchases of stocks at that time because the stock prices were incredibly low, and it was obvious that the prices will increase when the economy improved. Applying dollar-cost averaging at a time like that may have caused you to miss valuable money-making opportunities. Hence understanding when to apply this strategy and when to make large purchases are important skills that a new investor should develop.

How to Evaluate a Company

The following will provide you with some basic information on what to consider when evaluating a company.

1. Does the company have a proven track record of profitability? Profitability is an indicator of longevity. The company's financial reports called 10-K (annual financial report) and 10-Q (quarterly financial report) will provide comprehensive information on the company's financial standing. They can be found by going to Sec.gov and searching through the EDGAR database. Simply type the company's name in the search bar.

2. Does the company have network effects? Network effects refers to improvement in a product/service due to its use by many people. An example is TikTok.

3. Has the company's operations changed with the times in terms of technology, diversity, et cetera. Companies that do not evolve tend to die out eventually. E.g., Blockbuster failed to evolve with the rise of the internet and is currently out of business. Netflix evolved and is currently thriving. Other factors such as post-pandemic adjustments should be considered.

4. Does the company's management have a good track record? A manager that often misses the mark in critical areas such as improving on diversity and inclusivity in products, services, or employees may be setting themselves up to fail in the future. This should be a red flag for the new investor.

5. Is the founder the CEO? This is often a green flag. CEOs that are owners of the company tend to have a stronger drive to see the company succeed into the future. The thriving company, Berkshire Hathaway is led by its owner, Warren Buffett. However, a successor can also lead the company towards continued success.

6. Does the company's former employees leave bad reviews for the company on public forums? This is a red flag. The negative opinion of the employees can affect consumers' decision regarding whether they should continue to patronize or recommend the business.

7. Has there been a recent CEO employed to increase profit? This may be a red flag. A company that constantly changes CEOs to make profit may have bigger underlying structural and directional issues. Another red flag worth noting is when the CEO of the

business does not own any shares of the company he or she manages.

8. Has the company made a recent acquisition/merger that you do not trust? Acquisitions made by companies are expensive and may lead to layoffs or abandonment of the company's vision, negative change in company culture, legal risks, ineffective communication, or loss of good counsel.

9. Is the company stock fully valued? A fully valued stock is one in which price is believed to reflect the value of the company. A fully valued stock is less likely to experience significant increase in price. Undervalued or rapidly growing stocks are more advisable for a new investor.

10. Do you see the company growing or expanding in the future? This is important for obvious reasons. A company that is growing is more likely to experience significant increase in stock prices in comparison to a company that is not growing or expanding. Remember, some undervalued companies have low stock prices. For these companies, it is best to buy these stocks before their prices increase.

Here is a scenario to help you understand some of the concepts explained here.

Company XYZ1	Company XYZ2
Price per share is $100	Price per share is $50
Company is not meeting earnings expectations.	Company has been exceeding earnings expectations.
No growth, expansions, or technological advancement in recent times.	Is growing, expanding, and/or introducing modern technologies.
Public's perception of success is bleak.	Public's perception of success is high.

Figure 5: A comparison between two hypothetical companies.

If you are having a tough time recognizing that Company xyz2 is the right choice, trust me, you are overthinking it. The first thought that came to your mind was probably "duh!" If it was not, it should have been because as simple and basic as your decision to buy Company xyz2 stock was, that is exactly how simple and basic your investment decisions can be. Company xyz2 shows growth, innovation, and expansion. It is also a leader in its sector. These qualities make Company xyz2 stock the better option for an investor with little money to invest. Remember when we agreed that you will need common sense to succeed in the stock market?

Prior to investing in any fund, make sure that you understand the fund's risks, costs, and expenses. Such information can be found by reading the annual reports and prospectus provided by the fund's sponsor. Additional information may also be found on podcasts and website, some of which will be provided in a subsequent chapter, blogs, videos on social media, and magazines. Remember, losing some or all the money you invest into the stock market is a very real possibility. Funds invested in the stock market are not insured like the funds in a savings account at your local financial institution.

A simple table or excel sheet summarizing companies that you are interested in can be created as a guide to help you visualize which companies you might want to invest in.

Company	Capitalization	Debt to Equity Ratio	CEO Invested
XYZ 1	Large cap	Less than 1	Yes
XYZ 2	Mid cap	Greater than 1	No
XYZ 3	Small cap	Greater than 1	Yes

Figure 6: An example of a summary of results from researching companies.

How To Determine Valuation Using Price-to-Earnings Ratio

Knowing if a company is overvalued or undervalued is a crucial step to enable the investor to decide if they want to invest in a particular company. If a company is undervalued, then investing in that company gives the investor a good chance of making a good return on their investment because an undervalued company has growth potential. On the other hand, if a company is overvalued, investing in that company may be riskier as there is a chance that the company may be headed for a downturn. In which case, the investor stands a higher chance of losing their investment. This is not set in stone however, as there are some companies that are overvalued, but continue to grow, expand, and innovate. Despite this conflicting information, it is important for the investor to be able to determine if a company's stock is expensive relative to its earnings, and to predict the future earnings of the company. This can be determined by looking at the Price-to-Earnings ratio (P/E ratio).

P/E ratio shows how much investors are willing to pay per $1 of earnings. P represents the market price of a share. 'E' represents earnings per share in the last 12 months divided by the number of outstanding shares.

If a company's share is trading at $50 with earnings per share of $5, then the P/E ratio is 10. That means that the buyer of the share is willing to invest $10 for every $1 of earnings. This is the formula for P/E ratio:

$$P/E \text{ ratio} = \frac{\text{Market price per share}}{\text{Earnings per share}}$$

$$P/E \text{ ratio} = \frac{\$50 \text{ per share}}{\$5 \text{ per share}} = \frac{\$10}{\$1}$$

What the P/E Ratio Can be Used For

1. Determine stock valuation: if a company's P/E ratio is high when compared to that of the companies in its industry, which means that it has a high market price compared to earnings. If the P/E ratio is low compared to that of other companies, then it has higher earnings compared to market price. Which also means that the stock is undervalued in compared to that of other companies. High P/E ratio indicates that the company is considered a growth company, but low, the company is considered a value company.

2. Predict future returns: a value company with a low P/E ratio have an expectation of higher growth and higher earnings in the future. Hence, investors are willing to pay a higher price for the company's stocks.

3. Evaluate indexes: P/E ratio can be used to evaluate indexes such as the S&P 500. This was about 24 in March of 2022. This reflects the average of all the companies that are within the index. An investor may compare the P/E ratio of investments that track the S&P 500 with that of the S&P 500 in their decision-making process.

4. Compare stocks within the same industry: the P/E ratio of different stocks may be compared to determine the relative costs of the shares. This can provide the investor with information on whether the price of a particular share is high or low.

Note that performing calculations for P/E ratios as they are usually provided with stock price data on brokerage websites. For example, to find the P/E ratio of Amazon, simply go to a brokerage company, say, Fidelity.com and type amazon in the search bar. The PE ratio will be provided along with the stock price and other useful information.

Notes:

CHAPTER 7

How to Buy Your First Stock

Step1

Open your brokerage account. Go to a brokerage company's website It could be from the list provided below in chapter 9. Register and follow the prompts to open your account. You will need at least one form of identification. Linking your checking account may be needed to make transfers between your brokerage account and your regular checking account. Read every instruction provided carefully prior to opening your account to ensure that you are opening the right kind of account for your investment journey. For instance, do not open a retirement account if you mean to open a regular investment account that you can withdraw from at any time. Most retirement accounts do not permit withdrawals before age 65 without a penalty.

Step 2

Fund your brokerage account. On the website, find the link for transferring money and follow the prompts to transfer funds from your bank account to your brokerage account. The amount of money you transfer depends on how much you are willing to invest and how much the stocks you are interested in costs. The funds that are transferred must be invested. Uninvested funds do not experience stock market fluctuations and cannot be lost to the stock market because they are not yet part of the stock market. They are merely in the brokerage account. Some brokerages automatically sweep these uninvested funds into a form of savings account that generate some interest until the investor invests it.

Step 3

Buy stocks. Make sure that your funds have settled. Simply stated, make sure your funds are available to make purchases with. There is usually information regarding how much funds you have available to make purchases in the order section. Some brokerage firms require a longer length of time for deposited funds to settle in comparison to others. If your funds are not available to make purchases with, give it some time, think 2 to 5 business days. Every brokerage firm have rules regarding settlement times. Follow those rules to avoid any violations of the platform that you use. Violations may lead to fees or restrictions so read the rules carefully and follow them accordingly. If your funds are available to make purchases with, it's showtime! Ahem…that means it is time to buy some stocks.

To buy stocks, do the following:

1. Log in to the brokerage account you created.

2. Type the name of the company whose stock you intend to purchase in the search bar and click search. Once found, click on the company's name, or ticker symbol (see glossary). Once clicked, you should be able to see information about the stock such as the current trading price as well as other news about the company that owns that stock. You should also see buy or sell options.

3. Click on the applicable icon to buy and enter all required information such as the number of stocks you intend to purchase, the price at which you want your order fulfilled, transaction types: market order, limit order et cetera. (See glossary). Market orders and limit orders are the most common order types used by investors. Basically, a market order ensures that your order is fulfilled immediately at the current trading price. With a limit order, you set the price range at which the order is fulfilled. If you are purchasing a dividend paying stock, you may choose whether you want to reinvest your dividends. If you choose to reinvest your dividends, the gains will be added to the stock that generated it and become a part of your investment with that

company. It will not be paid into your investment account to be withdrawn. If you do not choose to reinvest your dividends, the dividend payouts will be paid into your investment account which you may transfer to your bank account.

4. You can choose how long you want your buy or sell order to stay open pending fulfillment before cancellation. These options are indicated by abbreviations such as GTC (Good till Cancelled), Day + ext. (Day plus Extended time), et cetera. See the glossary for their meanings. After your purchase order is placed, you will be able to view your pending order on the 'orders' page. On this page, once your order is fulfilled, you will see the "pending" status changed to "filled." The exact wording may be different from the ones given above. Voila! You own stocks! Piece of cake, isn't it?

It is highly recommended that you have up-to-date information about the companies whose stocks you own as that will guide your decisions regarding what future steps to take with the stock. Depending on the company's performance, you may choose to buy more of that stock, sell what you own, or hold it for a longer period. Remember, selling your stocks after holding it for less than a year may result in higher taxes for the investor. Research does not end when you purchase a company's stocks. It is advised that you continue to seek out news about the company in popular media outlets, social media, blogs and from the company's websites. You can also sign up for the company's newsletter.

Notes:

CHAPTER 8

Tips to Help You Succeed

1. Always buy low, hold, and sell high. The only way that you can grow your wealth is if you sell your investment at a higher price than your purchase price. Giving in to peer pressure or the fear of missing out can cause you to lose money. Use the same strategy that has been mastered by other more experienced investors. For example, when new investors hear fearful news about company xyz, they tend to become fearful of the company going bankrupt and sell while the price is high. Experienced investors on the other hand act differently. If the experienced investor believes that company will recover and continue to flourish, they will buy more of company xyz stocks while the stock price is down to increase their position with company xyz at a lower price. While the inexperienced investor may have made some gains by selling while the price is high, the experienced investor that added to their position while the price was down will make more gains when the stock price increases because they gained a higher position at a lower price.

2. Read and research. This is one of the most important things you can do on your investing journey. It is impossible to pick worthwhile

investments without some form of research involvement. Public companies are required to provide financial and other information to the public which investors can use to judge if they would like to invest in a particular company. In addition to having access to the financial information of public companies, investors can also obtain knowledge on who works in these companies, specifically, the CEOs of public companies. Understanding the leaders of a company and their track record can help the new investor in their research. CEOs of publicly traded companies are required to report anytime they purchase or sell their company's stock. This information can be used to determine how the CEO views the future performance of the companies they manage.

3. Platform penalties. They are penalties that can result from failing to follow the rules of your investment platform. Such penalties may be in the form of fees for good faith violations. They may also be in the form of trading restrictions whereby the investor is restricted from trading for some time depending on the rules of the brokerage firm. Good faith violation refers to when an investor purchases stock using money that is not readily available in their account. A trading restriction refers to an instance where an investor is restricted from trading for up to

90 days because of a violation or repeated violations within their investment account.

4. To maximize diversification within the stock market, consider large cap companies, small cap companies, and international companies as a part of your portfolio. Although owning an index fund that tracks the performance of the S&P 500 index is a less risky way for a new investor to grow wealth, the S&P 500 index fund contains large cap companies. There are other index funds and ETFs that contain small cap, mid cap, and international companies. There are also some mutual funds and individual stocks that can be purchased to increased diversification.

5. Examine your portfolio occasionally. Evaluate your holdings at least once a year to see when you need to rebalance your holdings by either selling a particular stock or adding to a particular stock. It is ill-advised to constantly analyze your portfolio as that can lead you to trade more often than you initially planned to. You can perform portfolio analysis yourself by checking your investments to determine if they are headed in the right direction. You may seek to answer questions such as, are your investments meeting your goals? Are they diversified enough? Are you over-diversified? Are fees negatively affecting your portfolio. There are many other questions you

may ask. There are online investment analysis tools that are available to help you gain insight into the performance of your portfolio. Companies such as Morning Star and Schwab have portfolio analyzers that allows an investor to input their data and track the performance of their investments. Analysis may be performed on individual stocks, the portfolio, or on the fees that are associated with your investment. The goal is to lower your risks and increase your returns.

6. Create your own qualification standards to use to determine if a company meets your requirements before you invest in their stock. For example, create a simple excel sheet and use qualifiers such as earnings, future growth, expansion, current and future profitability, debt, and capital to eliminate companies from your choices. You may choose to use a grading scale such as a scale from 1 to 10 with 1 being least likely to have a particular quality and 10 being most likely to have that quality. Or for example, you may group your tech company options into large and small with small being any technology company with less than $2 billion market capitalization and a big technology company being one with more than $2 billion market capitalization. Market capitalization refers to the market value of a publicly traded company based on its current share price and the number of outstanding

shares of the company. It is crucial to have a method for eliminating companies that do not meet your set criteria for investing.

7. Temperament. Being able to maintain an even keel regardless of the madness and fluctuations that may be happening in the stock market will enable you to make good decisions regarding your investment during tough economic conditions. This simply refers to one's ability to stay level-headed and logical rather than being swayed by the fear of losing one's money which can cause one to sell their stocks at a tough time. It is easier to remind oneself to remain logical when things are going smoothly than when there is high volatility. Remember that volatility is a normal part of a market cycle. A high stock volatility does not always mean considerable risk because, a company that has frequent fluctuations in price while having an upward trajectory provides the opportunity to buy in and increase one's holdings in the company. Volatility is a normal part of the stock market

8. Keep a close eye on fees. If your portfolio is managed by a professional, you will be charged fees. By keeping a close eye on any transaction fees or commissions associated with your account, you will gain more from the growth of your investments. While you do not have to avoid investing in securities with

fees to grow your wealth, it is advisable that you make sure that the securities you pick do not have high fees that can eat away at your earnings. Remember, fees may be charged when you buy, sell or exchange funds. Shop around before you decide on what security to buy. You may be able to find a similar stock with little or no fees. Fees may also be charged annually depending on the kind of investment you have. Fees are often explained in account opening documents, trade confirmations, account statements and many other financial documents that are associated with your investment account.

9. Opportunity cost. Even a basic understanding of what this means will guide you towards making decisions that are best for you and your financial future. In basic terms, opportunity cost means the cost of making a particular choice over another choice. For example, if you have $100 and you considered splurging your hard-earned money on drinks in a bar with your friends, but as you were about to get dressed, you get a notification on your phone about a reduction in price of stock xyz2 from $200 to $100. You then decide to purchase stock xyz2 with your $100, leaving you with no money to splurge on your friends. The opportunity cost of buying that stock is the drink you would have splurged on. If you decided to ignore the

notification and went ahead and splurged on your friends, the opportunity cost of that fun, alcohol-filled time you had with your friends will be the investment you did not make. Hence, it is best to consider the opportunity cost of every purchase made on your investment journey.

10. Avoid group think and herd mentality. If you want to achieve results that are better or different form that of the crowd, you must think and act differently. Put simply, if everybody is flocking to a particular stock, it is highly likely that the stock is overpriced, and it is the wrong time to buy. There is a common saying in the investing world that goes "Buy when there's blood on the streets." This means that investors should buy stocks when the economy is down, when other investors are in panic due to their loss in the stock market, when other investors are too afraid to buy because the economy is in an inflation or a recession, et cetera. A simple reason a down market such as a recession is the best time to buy is because, most stocks are at extremely low prices, and when the recession ends, the stock price will increase, thereby, increasing the wealth of the investor. If you have ever wondered why the rich get richer after poor economic conditions, natural disasters, and pandemics, while the poor get poorer, it is because when an occurrence such as a natural

disaster or a pandemic occurs, poorer people panic and worry and as a result, they hold unto the little that they have, to keep from running short just in case things get worse. Richer people on the other hand see the poor economic conditions as an opportunity to increase their wealth. They believe that the economy will improve in the future, so they use their money to invest more in areas that are most negatively affected by the downturn. So, when the economy improves, the poorer people that invested nothing are left with the little they had before the current economic upswing, while the rich people that invested during the downturn gain more wealth due to the upswing in the economy.

11. Know the difference between buying low and buying at the bottom. Buying low refers to buying a stock when its price is low compared to previous prices. While buying at the bottom refers to buying stocks when its price is at its lowest during a downturn. The bottom can only be identified in hindsight because nobody knows what the lowest price of a stock will be during a period of volatility. Hence, it is ill-advised to try to time the market perfectly to buy a stock at the bottom. It is a much better strategy to buy when the stock's price is low and reap the benefits of any further price increase. The same concept applies to selling a stock at the top. It is

difficult to know when a stock's price has reached its top except in hindsight. Hence, if an investor decides to sell a stock, it is better to sell it when the price is higher than the purchase price rather than wait for the price to reach the top. If the investor chooses to wait for the bottom before buying, or the top before selling, they risk missing opportunities to make high investment gains.

12. Judging a company's stock by price alone. If you are judging a company's stock by only the stock's positive price action, you are most likely buying at the top. If for instance, you learned about the company's upwards stock price movement and decide to purchase the stocks and ride it to the top, you stand the risk of buying the stock at the top or at a higher price than what it may be worth in the future. Usually, by the time a new investor notices the high price of a stock, the experienced investors will most likely have purchased the stock and driven the stock price upward. By the time the new investor decides to buy the stock, the price may have reached the top and is about to begin trending downwards. If the new investor buys the stock at the top, the downward trend that follows will cause the new investor to lose rather than gain. One way to know when the stock price may be approaching the top is that the average person will be talking about the stock. If you are on a

train or at work and the average person who knows little to nothing about the stock market or investing is talking about a particular stock, specifically, in the context that it is a good time to buy due to its growth, then it is very likely that the stock price may be at the top. Undervalued stocks, which are the best stocks to buy, do not get that much attention because, their low stock prices do not look as attractive to an inexperienced investor.

13. Until you are comfortable with your knowledge about investing, Tread lightly. Do not put all your money in a single company. No matter how little money you have invested. Remember to diversify across sectors. Also remember that an over-diversified portfolio mimics an index fund. Therefore, if you own an index fund, but would not like the rest of your portfolio to look like the same index fund that you already own, you should be conscious of how much you diversify. There is an abundance of information about stock investing which can be overwhelming for a new investor. Rather than trying to learn all that there is to know about investing in the stock market, learn as much as you need to take your first step and do the same for the next step and so on. For instance, you do not need to know which companies are the best investments before opening your brokerage account. Assuming

that your account is opened, you do not need to learn the differences between an individual stock and an index fund to fund your brokerage account. If you want to take baby steps at the start of your investing journey, you may begin investing safely by buying an Index fund or a mutual fund as your first or one of your first investments. They are slow to grow but have lower risk than any single company's stock. ETFs are the same, and in addition, they have some of the lowest investment fees, making them the obvious choice for many new investors.

14. Cash-Flow Positive. Before you choose to invest in a company, do some research on them to make sure that the company is cash flow positive. A company with positive cash-flow has more money flowing into the company than they do going out. A company that is cash flow positive can remain in business well into the future. On the other hand, negative cash-flow refers to a situation whereby, there is more money flowing out of the company than there is flowing in. A company that has negative cash-flow runs the risk of running out of money and not being able to sustain their business. Positive cash-flow is critical to a business' success for many reasons, some of which are; companies must be able to buy inventory, pay their employees, settle their debts, cover operating expenses,

reinvest into the business, and have a buffer against harsher economic times that may occur.

Notes:

CHAPTER 9

Resources for Success

You may use any of the following financial institutions to open your brokerage account:

1. www.vanguard.com
2. www.schwab.com
3. www.tdameritrade.com
4. www.fidelity.com
5. www.etrade.com
6. www.computershare.com
7. www.ally.com
8. www.betterment.com
9. www.m1finance.com
10. www.zachstrade.com
11. www.acorns.com
12. www.atom.com
13. www.tradestation.com
14. www.sofi.com
15. www.merrilledge.com
16. www.stash.com
17. www.axosbank.com
18. www.interactivebrokers.com
19. www.public.com
20. ww.gemini.com
21. Webull (app)
22. Robinhood (app)
23. Coinbase (app)
24. Banks such as Chase, Fifth Third, and Bank of America, et cetera.

Investment Podcasts for Your Motivation and Education

1. Be Wealthy and Smart
2. Millennial Investor
3. The investing for Beginners Podcast
4. Quick and Dirty Tips for a Richer Life
5. Sound Investing
6. Invest Like the Best
7. We Study Billionaires
8. Get Started: The Beginner's Guide to the Stock Market
9. Animal Spirits
10. Exchanges at Goldman Sachs
11. Equity Mates Investing
12. The Disciplined Investor
13. Best of US Investors Podcast
14. The Intelligent Investing Podcast
15. The Rich Dad Show
16. Investment Fund Secrets
17. The His and Hers Money Show
18. Fresh Invest
19. The Dave Ramsey Show
20. Mad Money with Jim Cramer
21. Motley Fool Money
22. Invest ED
23. The Meb Faber Show
24. Masters of Scale
25. The Peter Schiff Show
26. CNBC's Fast Money
27. The Journal
28. Stock Club

29. Marketplace
30. The Investor's Podcast Network
31. Pivot
32. Invest Like a Boss
33. Jill on Money
34. Stacking Benjamins
35. Fidelity Connects
36. The College Investor
37. Planet Money
38. Chit Chat Money
39. Wall Street Unplugged
40. Business Daily
41. FYI-For Your Innovation
42. Investing Insights
43. Value Investing with Legends
44. More Money Podcast
45. Money for the Rest of Us
46. Simple, but Not Easy
47. The Long View
48. 2050 Trailblazers
49. Rational Reminder
50. The Young Investors Podcast
51. The Contrarian Investor Podcast
52. Money to the Masses Podcast
53. Rule Breaker Investing
54. The Intellectual Investor
55. Value Investing with Legends
56. Life Kit: Money
57. The Money Tree Investing Podcast
58. The Radical Personal Finance
59. Shares for Beginners
60. Returns on Investment Podcast

Websites for Research

1. SEC.gov
2. Investor.gov
3. Wsj.com
4. Fool.com
5. Investopedia.com
6. Yahoo finance.com
7. Nerdwallet.com
8. Seekingalpha.com
9. Benzinga.com
10. Ivesting.com
11. Zack.com
12. Morningstar.com
13. Alphastreet.com
14. Marketwatch.com
15. Google Finance
16. Reddit.com
17. Equitymaster.com
18. Ragingbull.com
19. CNBC.com
20. Thestreet.com
21. Bloomberg.com
22. Foxbusiness.com
23. Barrons.com
24. Yieldstreet.com
25. Investmentnews.com
26. USnews.com
27. Nasdaq.com
28. Fortune.com
29. Businessinsider.com
30. MSN.com

Helpful Books on Investing

1. The Little Book of Common Sense Investing by John C. Bogle
2. Broke millennial by Erin Lowry
3. Thinking Fast and Slow by Daniel Kahneman
4. The Intelligent Investor by Benjamin Graham
5. Rental property Investing by Brandon Turner
6. Rich DAD Poor DAD by Robert Kiyosaki
7. The Money Manual by Mike Enemigo
8. Think and Grow Rich by Napoleon Hill
9. One Up on Wall Street by Robert Lynch
10. The Simple Path to Wealth by JL Collins
11. The Psychology of Money by Morgan Housel
12. The Millionaire Next Door by Thomas J Stanley and William D. Danko
13. A Random Walk Down Wallstreet by Burton G Malkiel
14. Richer, Wiser, Happier by William Green
15. The Early Investor by Michael W Zisa

CHAPTER 10

Common Questions and Answers

Here are some commonly asked questions and their answers that may be of benefit to you:

Q: Do I need a brokerage account to buy stock?

A: Yes. Your transactions will take place through your brokerage account. There are brokerage companies that provide the ability for everyone to open an investment account. Your regular bank next door such as Chase bank also provide investment services including the opportunity for people to buy stocks. As at this moment, you can purchase individual stocks at Computershare.com. However, prior investment information is required for initial signup.

Q: How much money do I need to buy a stock?

A: Some shares cost as little as $0.10. If you, say, open a Robinhood account and purchase a stock of company xyz through Robinhood, opening a Robinhood account will cost you $0.00, all you will need to buy one share of company xyz will be $0.10. Yes, 10 cents!

Have you slapped yourself on the forehead yet? You should have!

Q: Where can I find information about a company in which I am interested?

A: If your best friend is a human being, you are already headed in the wrong direction. The internet should be your best friend. To get the most up-to-date information about a company, look at the company's newsletters, read information on their website, as those contain current and future projects of said company, as well as the company's progress and expectations. But company's newsletters can be very biased in their favor, so visit websites that are not affiliated with the company in question. An example of places to gather information from are YouTube businessinsider.com, yahoo finance.com, news channel sites, and your favorite social media.

Q: Should I hire a stockbroker to purchase my stocks for me as I am inexperienced?

A: Hiring a stockbroker is not necessary for a beginner investor with little money. It is important to keep your cost as low as possible when starting your investment journey. It costs money to hire a stockbroker, plus, stockbroker fees are not dependent on the outcome of your investments. In other words, you will have to pay broker fees whether you gain or lose money in your investment. There are many apps and websites available that make investing easy with little to no fees. We have compiled a list of apps and websites that allows you to begin your investment journey (See chapter 9).

Q: Cheap or expensive stocks, which is a better buy?

A: The cost of a particular stock is not as important as the value of the company that owns said stock. Buying an expensive stock does not mean that the stock will appreciate better or faster than a stock that costs less. Your focus should be on buying stocks that have the potential to grow over time. Simply put, the price of the stock you choose to buy does not matter if you know that it is from a good company, and you can afford to buy it.

Q: Should I buy individual stocks, ETFs, Index funds, or Mutual funds

A: As a beginner investor, it is advisable that you choose an investment that is passive, less risky, affordable, and diversified. Hence, an S&P 500 ETF is an excellent choice but certainly not the only one.

Q: Can one become rich by investing in the stock market?

A: Many people believe the answer to this question to be 'no.' However, we believe the answer is 'most definitely'! But first, let us make sure that we have the same understanding of the word "rich". According to Merriam-Webster, rich means "having abundant possessions and especially material wealth." Investing can increase your material wealth and possessions and lead you to abundance if done correctly. Remember, if investing does not increase material wealth, there would be no such thing as investors, investing, the stock market, stocks, shares, an investing mogul called Warren Buffett…you get the idea!

Q: Should I invest all my money in the stock market?

A: Resounding NO! Under no circumstance is it advisable to put all your money into the stock market. Finding other avenues of investment that do not include the stock market is part of diversification, and it is particularly important for safeguarding against losing all your money when the stock market takes a turn for the worst. The more diversified your investment portfolio is in areas outside the stock market, the better positioned you will be to take risks in the stock market. Riskier investments can generate more wealth in comparison to less risky investments.

Q: How do I know when I am ready to begin investing?

A: If you follow the three steps mentioned in chapter 7, on how to begin your actual investment process, all you need to know is enough to take each step when the time comes. Nobody knows all there is to know about the stock market. You certainly do not need to learn all the complex inner workings of the stock market to get started on your investing journey. Analysis paralysis is a real thing. So, put simply, in the words of NIKE, "Just Do It". Or in this case, just begin and learn what you need to take the next step.

Notes:

Glossary

Stock Market Investing Terminology

401K: a workplace savings or investment plan for retirement.

10-K: comprehensive financial report filed annually by a publicly traded company as required by the U.S Securities and Exchange Commission (SEC).

10-Q: comprehensive financial report filed quarterly by a publicly traded company as required by the U.S Securities and Exchange Commission (SEC).

Asset: an item of value that can be exchanged for another item of value.

Bear Market: a market in which stock prices are falling, or when the S&P 500 falls by 20% or more from their peak. Buying stocks is encouraged in a bear market.

Bond: a loan from an investor to a borrower such as an institution. The institution may use the loan to fund its operations or other expansion projects while the investor receives income in the form of interest for providing the loan.

Bull Market: a market in which stock prices are rising. Selling or holding are encouraged in a bull market.

Capital: assets used in production e.g., cash or machinery.

Cash Flow: cash that is moving into and out of a business.

Commodity: an economic good such as raw materials or resources used in the production of goods and services.

Dead Cat Bounce: this is a jargon that refers to when a security or stock experiences a temporary recovery during a downward trend.

Diversification: the process of increasing the variety of sectors invested in.

Dividend: profits distributed to shareholders.

Dollar-Cost Averaging: the practice of investing a fixed dollar amount on a regular basis regardless of share price.

Equity: a share of a company's stock.

Expense Ratio: management fee paid by investors.

Exchange Traded Fund (ETF): a basket of financial assets that tracks or mirrors the performance of an index, commodity, or other assets.

Federal Interest rate (a.k.a Federal Funds Rate): the rate at which banks charge other banks in the process of borrowing and lending excess reserves from one another. The Federal Open Market Committee (FOMC) determine the rate.

Fund: money set aside for a specific purpose.

Growth fund: a portfolio of stocks that is focused on capital appreciation rather than dividend payouts.

Income fund: a portfolio of stocks that is focused on income in the form of interests or dividends rather than capital appreciation.

Index: an indicator or the ruler with which market performance is measured E.g., the S&P 500 index.

Index fund: a fund that tracks the performance of a particular index. E.g., An S&P 500 index fund tracks the performance of the companies in the S&P 500 index.

Inflation: decline of purchasing power of a particular currency.

Investment: an asset acquired with the goal of generating income or earning profit.

Liquidity: the ease with which an asset can be converted into cash.

Load: this is the fee paid by investors to purchase or sell a particular investment.

Market Capitalization: stock price multiplied by the number of outstanding shares.

Market value: the price that buyers are willing to pay for an asset.

Mutual fund: an investment strategy that pools together money from different people and invests it in stocks, bonds, and other securities.

Nasdaq: a stock exchange designed to allow for the electronic trading of stocks.

New York Stock Exchange (a.k.a NYSA):

Opportunity Cost: the value of what is not chosen from a group of two or more possible alternatives.

Price-to-Earning (P/E) Ratio: this is the company's stock price divided by the company's earning. Investors use this information to determine whether to invest in a company. A high ratio is an indication that the stock price is higher than the company's earnings. Low ratio signifies a possibly undervalued company. It may also be an indication of slower growth.

Portfolio: a collection of financial investments such as stocks, bonds, cash, and other assets.

Principal: the original sum committed to the purchase of an asset, excluding added interests.

Risk: uncertainty with respect to an investment.

S&P 500: Standard and Poor's 500 is a collection of 500 of the largest publicly traded companies in the U.S stock market.

Security: an exchangeable financial asset that has value E.g., government bonds and shares.

Share: a single unit of ownership of a company.

Short-Selling (a.k.a Shorting): this refers to a process whereby, an investor borrows socks from a broker and sells them with the expectation that the price of the stock will fall in the future, and the investor will buy back the stock at the cheaper price and return them to the broker.

Stock: a security that represents an ownership of a piece of a company. Also known as shares.

Stockholder (a.k.a Shareholder): refers to any person, or institution that owns at least one share of a company.

The Federal Reserve System (a.k.a The Fed): this is the Central bank of the United States. It is the bank for other banks. It engages in a wide variety of activities to maintain central control of the financial industry.

Volatility: refers to the sharp rise and fall of prices of securities in the stock market.

Yield: refers to the earnings realized from an investment over a period.

Investment Fees Terminology

401(k) fee: an administrative fee paid by the plan participants for the maintenance of the plan. It is often passed to the plan participants by the employer.

Expense Ratio: expense ratio fees may be charged by index funds, mutual funds, and exchange traded funds as a percentage of your investment for the operation of the fund.

Gross Expense Ratio (GER): this refers to the total annual expenses incurred in the operation of a fund.

Inactivity fee: fees charged to an investor for an inactive brokerage account.

Management or Advisory fee: a fee paid by an investor to a financial advisor. This is typically a percentage of assets under management.

Mutual fund transaction fee: fees charged when mutual funds are bought or sold.

Net Expense Ratio: gross expense ratio minus waivers and reimbursements. This refers to the cost of operating a fund without brokerage costs.

Sales Load: a charge or commission on some mutual funds, paid to the broker who sold the fund.

Trade commission: a brokerage fee that the new investor may pay for buying or selling stock.

Types of Orders

Market order: an order to buy or sell a security immediately. A market order is not always the last price at which the security traded. Prices often fluctuate so the last price that the security traded at may be different from the current trading price. A market order guarantees that the order will be executed at whatever the current price is at the time the trade is executed.

Limit order: this refers to an order to trade a security at a specific price or price range. When buying stock, an investor can set a limit on how high or low they would like for the price of a stock to be before it is executed. For example, if a buy order is placed with a limit order of $50.23 on stock A, that order will only be purchased if the price of stock A is $50.23 or lower. The order request will not be executed if the stock price is higher than $50.23. Hence when a limit buy order of $50.23 is placed to buy a stock that is, say, $50.24, or more, the order will remain pending until stock A is trading at $50.23 or lower.

Stop order (a.k.a Stop-loss order): this refers to an order to buy or sell a stock when the value of the stock reaches a specific price. For example, when an investor that owns a stock trading at $50 sets a stop-loss order to sell a stock at $45, the order will be executed when the price reaches $45 or lower than $45 but not above $45. This ensures that the investor sells the security when the price drops below the price at which they would like to own it.

Buy stop order: this refers to an order that requests that a security be bought at any price until the security reaches the specified price, usually above the market price. For example, when a stock is selling at a market price (current price) of $50, a buy stop order at $55 is a request that the stock be purchased when the price is at any price up to $55. At $55.01 and above, the stock will not be purchased. This limits the amount of money that is spent on purchasing a particular stock.

Common Transaction Types

Day: this means that your order to trade stocks will be executed anytime within regular market hours, typically from 9:30am to 4:00pm ET in the U.S stock market for that day only.

Day Plus Ext.: this means day plus extended hours. With this, your order will be active and can be executed at any time between the regular day hours of 9:30am to 4:00 pm and the after-hours which typically spans from 4:00am to 8:00am ET and 4:00pm to 8:00pm ET for that day only.

GTC: this means good till cancelled. With this, an order will remain active during regular open market hours which range from 8:00am to 4:00 pm ET until the trade request is executed or cancelled by the investor. GTC orders are cancelled automatically after 90 days with most accounts if the trade is not executed within 90 days.

GTC Plus Ext.: this means good till cancelled plus extended hours. With this, a buy or sell order will remain active during regular open market hours which range from 9:30am to 4pm ET, including extended hours typically from 4:00pm to 8:00pm until the order is filled or cancelled. GTC plus Ext orders are cancelled automatically after 90 days with most accounts if the trade is not executed within 90 days.

Ext. (AM): morning extended hours typically spans from 4:00 am to 8:00am ET.

Ext. (PM): evening extended hours typically spans from 4:00pm to 8:00pm ET.

www.ingramcontent.com/pod-product-compliance
Lightning Source LLC
Chambersburg PA
CBHW070254220526
45465CB00004B/1620